EARLY IMMIGRATION IN THE UNITED STATES

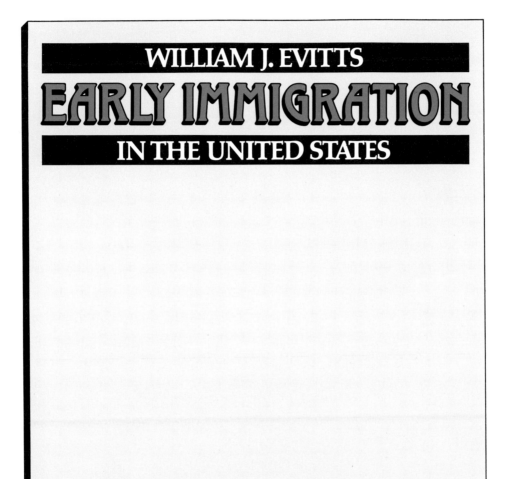

WILLIAM J. EVITTS

EARLY IMMIGRATION

IN THE UNITED STATES

Franklin Watts
New York / London / Toronto / Sydney
A First Book / 1989

Cover photo courtesy of: The Granger Collection

Photographs courtesy of: The Granger Collection: pp. 8, 13 (top and
bottom), 14, 15, 16, 17, 18, 20, 22, 26, 28 (top and bottom), 30 (top
and bottom), 33, 35, 36, 37, 39, 45, 46, 49, 52, 53, 59;
New York Public Library Picture Collection: p. 25; The New York
Historical Society: p. 41; UPI/Bettmann Newsphotos: p. 55.

Library of Congress Cataloging-in-Publication Data
Evitts, William J., 1942–
Early immigration in the United States / by William J. Evitts.
p. cm. — (A First book)
Bibliography: p.
Includes index.
Summary: Describes the United States as a nation of immigrants and the
reasons why people came to America, examining how the early immigrants,
from the Dutch to the Africans, settled and adapted to their new home.
ISBN 0-531-10744-2
1. United States—Emigration and immigration—History—Juvenile
literature. 2. Immigrants—United States—History—Juvenile
literature. [1. United States—Emigration and immigration—History.
2. Immigrants—United States—History.] I. Title. II. Series.
JV6451.E95   1989
325.73—dc19   88-34544   CIP   AC

CONTENTS

EARLY IMMIGRATION IN THE UNITED STATES

*Millions of immigrants came to the
United States between 1820 and 1930
seeking freedom and opportunity.*

1
A NATION OF IMMIGRANTS

All Americans are the children or grandchildren or great-great-great grandchildren of immigrants. An immigrant is a person who goes to another country to live permanently. The United States is a nation of immigrants. Only the Indians have been in America long enough to be called true Native Americans.

Why did immigrants come here? What would make a person, a family, or a whole community pack up all their things and move far away to a new land across the ocean?

For the millions of people who came to America, there were basically only two reasons. Some came because they simply could not stay where

How many immigrants came to the U.S.?
When did they come?
Where did they come from?

In 1790, the new United States government took the first careful census, or count, of the American people. Except for Africans and Indians, all Americans or their ancestors came from northern Europe.

- Two of every three from England
- One of every five from Africa
- The rest mainly from Scotland, Ireland, and Germany, followed by Holland and France

In the nineteenth and early twentieth centuries, immigrants were from

- Germany, almost six million
- Italy, almost five million
- Ireland, over four and a half million
- Austria and Hungary, over four million
- Britain (England, Scotland, and Wales), over four million
- Scandinavia (Norway, Sweden, Denmark, and Finland), over two million

they were any longer. Perhaps they lost their land, or years of bad harvests were starving them, or maybe they were rebels against their government. Others came to America not because home was so bad, but because the promise of the new land seemed so good. The United States was a land of opportunity and freedom.

Each immigrant, and each immigrant's family, had a different story. In the great age of immigration, from 1820 to 1930, more than thirty-seven million people came to America. This was the largest movement of people in the history of the world, and it made America what it is today.

2

A NEW WORLD

A "new world"—that is what America was to the early immigrants. It was a new place to start over, to find adventure and fortune, to be free.

Christopher Columbus "discovered" the New World in 1492. (Of course, the Native Americans already lived here, but Europeans did not really know of this land until Columbus returned from his voyage.) In the next century explorers came, then a few settlers and missionaries, mostly from Spain and Portugal.

The first permanent settlement in North America was Spanish. It was established in 1565 at St. Augustine, Florida. Then, in 1607, the English

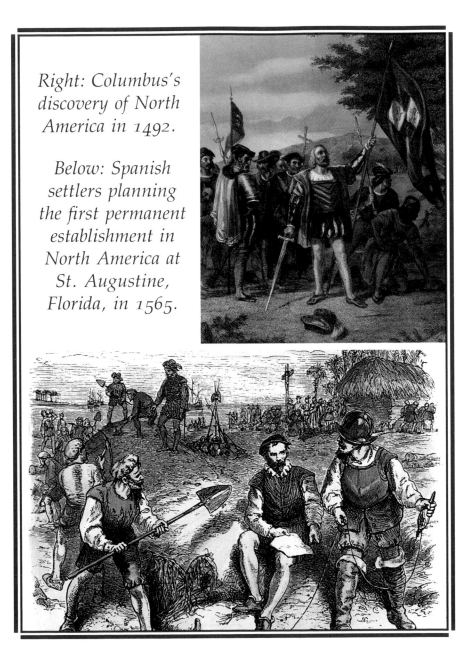

Right: Columbus's discovery of North America in 1492.

Below: Spanish settlers planning the first permanent establishment in North America at St. Augustine, Florida, in 1565.

*The English built a colony at
Jamestown, Virginia, in 1607.*

started the colony of Jamestown, Virginia. (A colony is a settlement controlled by another country).

Land was plentiful and cheap, so the English immigrants became farmers. They learned to grow tobacco. The chance to become a wealthy farmer with lots of land was an opportunity that most people could not hope for back in England. English immigrants also settled in Maryland, North and South Carolina, and Georgia.

Other English immigrants came to the New World to be free to worship God as they wished. They were called "Pilgrims" and "Puritans." The

Many English immigrants became wealthy farm owners soon after they settled the fertile land in Maryland, Virginia, North and South Carolina, and Georgia.

*In 1620, many English immigrants left their
homeland to escape religious persecution
and settled in Plymouth, Massachusetts.*

area where these religious immigrants settled was called New England. It was first settled in 1620, at Plymouth, Massachusetts.

Aside from the English, the most immigrants in colonial America came from Germany. The Germans settled in farm communities and mostly kept to themselves. They had their own churches, spoke German at home, and sometimes angered the English by the way they refused to become like the other colonists.

A group of Germans leave Chicago to settle in Colorado.

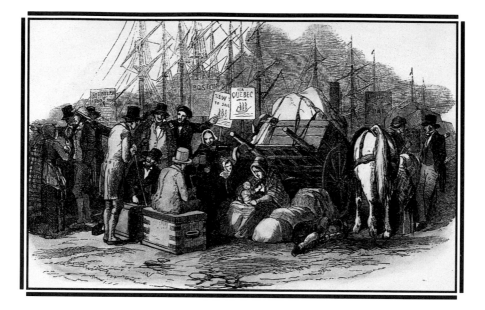

*The Irish came to America in large numbers,
hoping to find a better life.*

Next to the Germans, the largest group of immigrants in colonial times were the "Scotch-Irish," so called because they were originally from Scotland but they lived in northern Ireland. Ireland was a poor country, and the Scotch-Irish immigrants were looking for a better life in America.

There were other nationalities in colonial America—Swedes, Welsh, Irish Catholic, Dutch, and French. Most of these groups were small.

By the time the English colonies in North America became the United States of America, the pattern of immigration was clear. People came because opportunity was here. There was land and room to live as you wished and to worship as you pleased.

But there was a dark side to immigration too. The English immigrants who controlled society and government in America expected the newcomers to learn to speak English and be a part of the country. Other immigrants were welcome for the work they could do. But they weren't trusted.

These two ideas—that immigrants were welcome, but that people did not completely trust them until they became "like us"—come up again and again in American history.

And what of a special group of "immigrants" who had the hardest time of all in the early years of the United States? These people were almost one-fifth of the American population at the time of the Revolution, but theirs was a special case. They were not white Europeans, but captives from Africa. They were slaves, carried away to the New World against their will. Although these people didn't come here by choice as others did, they are an important group who helped make this country what it is.

Africans were brought to America
—against their will—to work as
slaves on vast plantations.

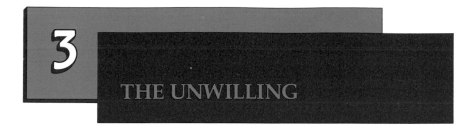

3

THE UNWILLING

The Africans came in chains. They were slaves. They were brought from their homes in Africa to work in the fields of America. With their strong hands and backs and spirit, they helped to build America.

Some of the white immigrants from Europe saw the dark-skinned Africans as different. They did not treat the Africans as people. They did not understand African culture or art or politics. They just saw slavery as a cheap and easy way to have enough workers for their large farms known as plantations.

*African slaves were treated cruelly.
In the scene above, a slaveowner sells
a family at a slave auction in Virginia.*

Many Africans were captured and forced onto ships that sailed to America. Those who survived the journey across the Atlantic were sold. Men were sold for hard work in the field. Women were sold to be house servants, cooks, and seamstresses. The children were bought to do odd jobs and then to grow into strong adults.

In time these forced immigrants mastered many skills. They became blacksmiths, carpenters, bookkeepers, wagonmasters, riverboat pilots, and more. Whatever work had to be done, the slaves did it.

Three-quarters of a million Africans lived in the United States in 1790. By 1860 that number was four and a half million. Four million of those were slaves; the rest were free.

Slavery was allowed in parts of this country until 1865, the year the Civil War ended. Almost all the people from Africa came to America before that time, and the great majority of them came here before 1800. Afro-Americans, as these unwilling immigrants came to be called, are among the oldest immigrant groups in the United States. They have had a powerful effect on American life, society, politics, and art.

4

THE FLIGHT
OF THE PEASANTS

The peasants of Europe were driven off the land there. They could not make a living on the tired soil any longer. New laws taxed their farms and they could not pay. There were too many people trying to live on too few acres. They were living in huts, eating poorly, and barely getting by. The peasants fled to the nearby cities or to America.

Not every immigrant was a peasant who had to leave the land. Some were skilled workers—carpenters, masons, boatbuilders, toolmakers. Others were shop owners, teachers, cooks. All wanted a better life in America.

News spread of people who had gone to America. Immigrants sometimes wrote back about their new lives in the New World. Sometimes American businesses advertised in Europe, asking for immigrants to come and work. The advertisements promised wonderful chances for a good life in America.

A poor Irishman reads a poster advertising immigration to America.

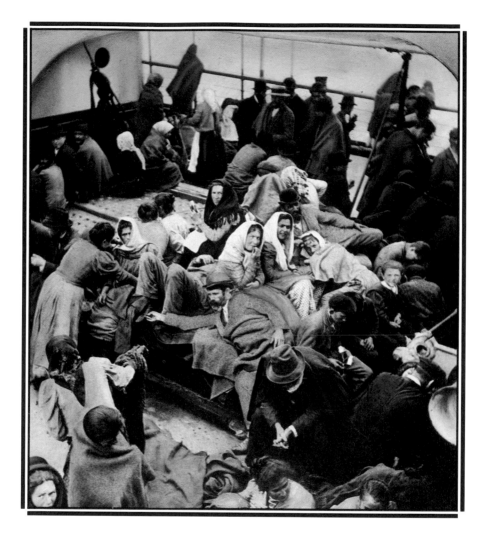

*Immigrants faced a difficult journey
to the "land of opportunity." Ships
sailing to America were cramped, and
the voyage was long and exhausting.*

It was hard to get to America. You needed at least a little money to buy meals on the way and to pay for the passage on the ship. Immigrants would sell all that they could to raise money. Sometimes a family would pool together all their money to send just one person to this country. In time, if that person made good, he or she could send money back for the others to come.

The voyage to America could be as harsh for the immigrants as the life they were trying to escape. The ships were cramped and dirty. Many people became sick. The dangerous journeys lasted weeks, sometimes more than a month.

After this long voyage, land was a welcome sight to the travelers. They probably landed at one of the great seaports like New Orleans, Baltimore, Philadelphia, Boston, and, busiest of all, New York City. These were big cities, crowded and strange to the peasants from Europe. As they looked ashore from the boat, the immigrants felt the excitement of being at last in the land of opportunity. But they also felt the fear of starting over in a strange place.

Immigrants could not just walk off the boat and up the street to a new life. They gathered their goods and collected the family around them. Then they waited on the boat or in special buildings on shore that sometimes looked like jails. This was a

When immigrants finally sighted land, they experienced overwhelming feelings of relief, excitement, and fear.

Left: At first, the big, busy cities seemed very strange to newly arrived immigrants.

period called "quarantine." The officials in America needed to check to see that everything was in order. They asked so many questions.

"Where did you come from?" the travelers were asked.

"Can you work, or will you become a beggar?"

"How much money do you have, and where did you get it?"

"Is someone meeting you? Do you have family here? Do you have a job waiting, a skill, a place to go?"

For immigrants who spoke no English, a translator had to be found to get the questions and answers from one language to the other and back again.

So many questions. So many forms to fill out. So many lines to stand on. Wait here. Stand over there. Be patient. Do as you are told.

In New York City, where huge numbers of immigrants entered the United States, an entire island in New York harbor, Ellis Island, was set aside just to receive them. Ellis Island became the first American stop for millions of immigrants from Europe. Some only stayed a day or two. They were the lucky ones. Their papers were in order. Their fam-

ilies or friends were there to take them to a home. They were healthy and had a little money. Other less fortunate immigrants could spend a month or more in the grim red-brick buildings of Ellis Island. Up and down the American coastline were similar stations, some large and some tiny, where the weary immigrants squeezed through the narrow opening into America.

Top left: Millions of immigrants arrived at New York City's Ellis Island.
Bottom: This photograph, taken in 1900, shows immigrants in the dining hall on Ellis Island.

5

STARTING OVER

How do you start over in a new land? What do you do if you don't speak the language, don't know the customs, and don't even know your way around?

The easiest way for immigrants to start over in America was to have friends or family already here. Lots of immigrants came to America because someone they knew had come before and had sent for them. Sometimes entire villages in Europe came to the United States, one family at a time.

Sometimes the immigrant was helped by an Immigrant Aid Society. These societies were in most major cities. They were made up of other immigrants, or businesses that wanted the immigrants to come work for them, or church people who just wanted to help.

Even if the immigrant had no family and no one he or she knew personally, there were bound to be others from the old country in every port city. The immigrants had the poorest neighborhoods with the smallest, oldest houses, usually near the docks where the immigrants arrived. It was a great comfort to immigrants to find people who knew their

The photograph below shows an ethnic immigrant neighborhood on New York City's Lower East Side.

home and language, and who understood what they were going through.

After 1820, "ethnic" neighborhoods (neighborhoods where people from a certain country gathered to live) began to appear in the big seaport cities of the United States. Before the Civil War the big ethnic groups were German, Irish, and Scandinavian. In their neighborhoods you could find churches, newspapers, social clubs, schools, and stores where the old language was still used and the old customs and foods were still known and understood.

A large number of immigrants had been farmers in their old country. In America most of them never left the port city in which they arrived. Jobs were in factories and shops, not out on the farms. Broke, unsure of where to go or how to get there, many immigrant farmers from Europe were forced to be city laborers in America in order to earn a living.

The cities became very crowded. It was hard to find a place to live. Many immigrants lived in huge buildings called tenements. Families were crammed into small apartments in these tenements. There was no indoor plumbing or heat. There was no yard, no open space, no fresh air.

Most immigrants took jobs as factory or sweatshop workers in the port city where they had landed.

*Immigrant families lived in cramped tenement
apartments with poor living conditions.*

City life was hard on the immigrants. They
moved from job to job. Everybody worked, even
the children. They worked in clothing factories, in
iron foundries, on the docks unloading ships, anywhere there was a job.

The children went to school when they were
able. They often had to put up with a lot of teasing
and abuse for being different, for being poor, and
for not speaking English very well. Many children
grew up speaking two languages. In school and on

the street, they used English. At home, with parents and grandparents in the crowded apartment, they spoke German or Polish or whatever was the language of the old country.

It was difficult for the immigrants to keep their families together. They all worked very hard, six days a week, ten to twelve hours a day. When the children were free from work, school, and chores,

Although children often worked in factories
with their families, they were expected
to attend school whenever possible.

they were out in the city streets learning the ways of the new land.

The immigrants would get together at church or maybe at a social club made up of other immigrants. There they could relax and talk about the old country. The women would shout back and forth as they hung the wash out to dry in the narrow alleys between the tenements. The men would smoke and occasionally go to the corner tavern to share their troubles with the other men.

As time went by, one immigrant group would slowly become wealthier and begin to move out of the "ghetto," as these ethnic neighborhoods were called. As one ethnic group moved out, another newer group would move in. The Germans who came in the 1820s might be replaced in the old neighborhood by the Irish in the 1840s. As the Irish became wealthier, the Italians might be the next group to move in. Some neighborhoods stayed the same for a long time. But other neighborhoods saw one group after another begin their new life in America there.

There were immigrants who escaped the port cities and traveled west to other towns where new industries needed workers. Cities like Pittsburgh, Cleveland, Buffalo, Cincinnati, St. Louis, and Chicago attracted many immigrants. All of these cities, and many more, have rich ethnic traditions.

Some immigrants left the port cities to go out and be part of the huge construction gangs that built America in the nineteenth century. Between 1800 and 1850, many miles of boat canals were built to haul heavy cargo across long distances. The Erie Canal went all the way across the state of New York, hundreds of miles from Albany, on the east, to Buffalo, on the west. The Erie Canal was dug by hand, by men using pick and shovel. Most of those men were immigrants.

Immigrants who left the port cities where they had entered the U.S. became "the builders of America." Many immigrant workers constructed the Erie Canal in Lockport, New York.

Between 1830 and 1900, hundreds of thousands of miles of railroad track were laid from coast to coast. The railroad officials hired tens of thousands of immigrant laborers. Some railroads even advertised in Europe for workers to come to America. On the West Coast, Chinese immigrants did a lot of the work building railroads.

Some new states and territories in the West wanted immigrants to come and be farmers. Sometimes these states would try to help the immigrants move out to the West or Midwest. Land was cheap, and the immigrant might get free transportation to go west. In 1861 the United States passed the Homestead Act, which gave away land to farmers who would settle on it. Many immigrants moved west to get this land and start up farms.

Just as there were immigrant neighborhoods in cities, there were immigrant farm communities. Foreigners who left the city to be farmers would look for places where their countrymen lived. They also looked for land that was like the land they

Many advertisements encouraged immigrants to move west.

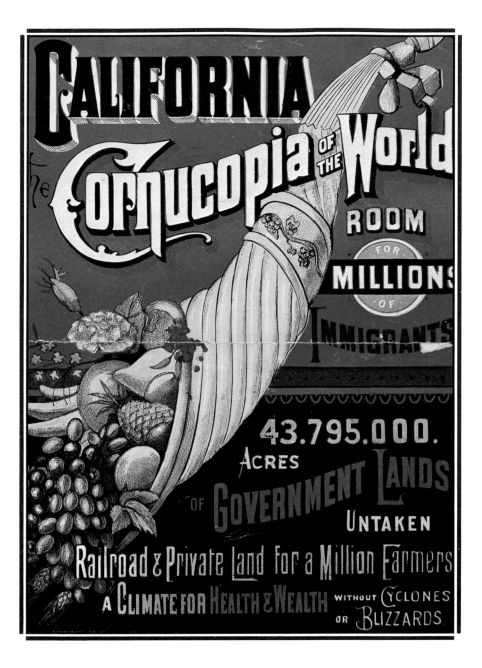

knew in the old country. German farm communities in the eighteenth century were on rolling, hilly land with good soil, just like in Germany, from south central Pennsylvania to the Carolinas, near the Blue Ridge Mountains. Norwegian and Swedish farmers in the nineteenth century set up towns in the cold northern plains, in Minnesota and the Dakotas.

If immigrants were needed in the West, and if land was cheap, why did so many immigrants stay in the cities? It was because it cost money to move and start farming. Houses and barns had to be built. Horses, cows, seed, and tools had to be bought. The family had to live until the first harvest came in. Then, too, by the last part of the nineteenth century, farming itself had become a very hard way to make much money. Prices for farm products were low and getting lower. Some immigrants looked wearily at the distance, the cost, and the risk of farming, and just stayed in the cities.

As the children of the immigrants grew up, they learned new ways. They were not peasants. They did not remember the old country and the old customs. Some of them became embarrassed by their parents and grandparents who still spoke with an accent and who liked to wear the old-fashioned clothes of their home country. These children preferred the ways of America.

6

AN UNCERTAIN WELCOME

America held out a welcome to the desperate peasants of Europe, to the ambitious young people who saw no hope in the Old World, and to those whose religion or beliefs made them unpopular. America had the Declaration of Independence and the Bill of Rights. America invited immigrants and was proud that all the world seemed to want to come to this land.

But the immigrants had a hard time here. They were different, and their ways were not understood. They were not trusted. This lack of trust caused problems.

One problem was differences in religion. Most Americans belonged to a group of Christian churches called Protestant churches. Many immigrants were not Protestants, but Roman Catholics, especially the Irish and the Italians. Protestants were suspicious of Catholics, whose church leader was the Pope. They thought that Catholics would be loyal to the Pope, not to the United States.

Jobs were another problem. When jobs were scarce, it made people angry to see thousands of new workers coming to America. These new workers took jobs that other people wanted. Because immigrant workers were hungry and broke and often desperate, they would work more cheaply than anyone else.

Sometimes a boss would fire all his American workers and replace them with immigrants who would accept lower wages. This would happen most often when workers were trying to organize as a group to get better wages and working conditions. These groups, called labor unions, would go on strike and refuse to work. When that happened, the bosses would fill the vacant jobs with new immigrant workers and keep the factories running. The workers on strike would attack the immigrants and beat them up for taking away their jobs and ruining their chance for better wages.

*Pennyslvania miners exercising
their right to vote*

Politics was a problem too. In the big cities, the immigrant neighborhoods had a lot of people who could vote. If they all stuck together and voted the same way, they could control the politics of a city. In fact, this did happen at times, and it made some people very angry at the immigrants.

Perhaps the biggest problem of all was simply that immigrants were *different*. Their language,

Since immigrants stuck together to survive in their new surroundings, they became unpopular with the Know-Nothing party—a political group who wanted to stop immigration. The political cartoon above illustrates the Know-Nothing party's belief that Irish and German immigrants were trying to steal elections and control big-city politics.

food, customs, and dress were strange. Some Americans who were born here had a hard time accepting those differences.

So the immigrants were caught in a trap. Americans expected immigrants to stop acting "foreign" and be "American, like us." Yet the Americans sometimes made it hard for immigrants to be a part of life in the United States. The immigrants made other people suspicious because they stuck together so much, but immigrants stuck together because it was the best way to survive in America.

The United States is a nation of immigrants, and immigrants have been more welcome here, in larger numbers, than anywhere else on earth. But some Americans have wanted to pass laws that make it hard, or impossible, for more immigrants to come here. In the 1850s, when immigration was very heavy, a political party grew up around the idea of stopping immigration. Its official name was the American Party, but for a long time it was called the Know-Nothing Party. It got this name because many of its members tried to keep the party a secret, and if asked about it, they would say, "I know nothing." The American Party did well in a few elections, and they proved that a lot of people did not like immigrants.

7

NEW IMMIGRANTS

After the Civil War (1861–1865), Americans began to talk about the "new" immigrants. The "old" immigrants were from northern Europe and Britain. Most of them were Protestant, except the Irish. The new immigrants were from southern and eastern Europe. They were more often Catholic, or Jewish, and seldom could speak any English. With their colorful clothes and unfamiliar customs, they seemed stranger and more "un-American" than the old immigrants.

The largest group of new immigrants was the Italians. Since 1880, over five million Italians have moved to the United States.

After 1865, new groups of immigrants began to arrive in the U.S. This photograph shows an Italian family on the ferry from Ellis Island to Manhattan.

Other big groups of new immigrants were the Poles, the Hungarians, the Russians, the Slavs (a group of people from eastern Europe who lived in several countries there), and many Jews, especially from Russia. Chinese immigrants also came to the United States.

Late in the nineteenth century, a group of immigrants arrived from the Ukraine, a place in eastern Europe, near Russia. Their story is a good example of the life of the new immigrants.

An American in Europe had talked the Ukrainians into coming to America. The man was an agent for a coal mine in Pennsylvania, rounding up laborers in Europe. He told the Ukrainians they would find jobs in America.

When they got to New York, speaking no English at all, the Ukrainians could not even find a place to stay. Their colorful clothes made people stare at them. They started to walk all the way to western Pennsylvania.

No one would give the Ukrainians a place to stay because they were afraid to take in such odd-looking people. The Ukrainians had no American money to stay in a hotel. A kindhearted American in Harrisburg, Pennsylvania, gave them food. A farmer let them sleep in his barn one night, but threw them out the next day. One night they slept under a bridge for shelter.

Finally, they reached Shenandoah, Pennsylvania, and met an American who was an immigrant from Lithuania, which is near the Ukraine. He understood their problem and took care of them.

These people got jobs in the mines, but probably did not understand that the mine owners were using them to break a strike by the other miners. The striking miners, many of whom were Irish, were angry at the Ukrainians, and fights broke out. It took a long time for the Ukrainians to make a peaceful home in the shanty village at the edge of town.

The Jews who arrived in great numbers late in the nineteenth and early in the twentieth century faced a special problem. Since they were not Christians, they were considered especially unusual. There was a great deal of prejudice against the Jews, even more than against other European immigrants. One thing that helped them to get by is that the Jews were one of the best educated groups ever to come to America.

Of all the immigrants, probably no one was treated more unfairly than the Chinese, who came

*In the late nineteenth century, there was
much prejudice against immigrants because
of their different beliefs and customs.
This political cartoon shows many groups
as "unwelcome guests" in America.*

to the West Coast. (This does not include the treatment of the people from Africa.) A few Chinese came during the Gold Rush of 1849. By 1880, more than one hundred thousand Chinese lived in America, mostly in California.

Like immigrants from Europe, the Chinese came because they were starving at home. Like the Africans, they suffered because they were of a dif-

Chinese immigrants were treated unfairly in America. Here they are shown undergoing inspection at the U.S. Customs House in San Francisco.

ferent race than most Americans. The work the Chinese found in America was hard labor in the mines, and in building the railroads of the West.

By the late nineteenth century, so many immigrants were coming to the United States from so many different places that Americans began to be afraid of what was happening. Some Americans attacked immigrants because of prejudice and fear.

The Chinese were often victims of violence. A mob murdered twenty-eight Chinese in Rock Springs, Wyoming, in 1885, for example, and burned down all the Chinese homes and businesses. Chinese immigrants found it almost impossible to find a place to live outside their ethnic neighborhoods. Many American cities today have "Chinatown" districts because for so long the Chinese could not live anywhere else.

Other immigrants were the victims of violence too. In 1891, eleven Italians were killed by a lynch mob in New Orleans, and several more by a mob in the mining regions of Colorado.

The Chinese were the first group to have a law passed against them, saying no more could come to the United States. This happened in 1882. By 1917 the United States was ready to limit *all* immigration. In that year the government began to pass laws that controlled how many immigrants could come to the United States, and from which countries they could come. By 1920 even tougher laws were passed. The great century of immigration was coming to an end.

Today immigration into the United States is controlled by law. The laws say how many immigrants are allowed into the country. Each country or region of the world is allowed a quota. It takes a

Today America is a land of immigrants. Although people still try to come to this country, there are strict laws making immigration to the U.S. very difficult.

lot of paperwork and patience to move to the United States now. A big government agency, the Immigration and Naturalization Service, looks after all that paperwork and all those laws.

Yet hundreds of thousands, perhaps millions, of immigrants still come to America each year. They come from the Caribbean and from Central America. They come from Asia. If they cannot enter the country legally, they try to smuggle themselves in.

America, it seems, is still the land of hope and opportunity. We are still a nation of immigrants.

8 AMERICA AND THE IMMIGRANT

The poet Walt Whitman said that America is "a nation of nations." The family and town names in the United States tell you that the people came from all over the world. Venice is in Italy, Moscow is in Russia, Paris is in France, Dublin is in Ireland, Glasgow is in Scotland, Warsaw is in Poland, Athens is in Greece—but these are all town and city names in the United States too. Look in the telephone book and you will find names from around the world— German names, English names, Italian and Irish and Chinese and Polish names, to list just a few.

The way the immigrants became Americans was pretty much the same, no matter where the immigrants came from. The first generation, the ones who crossed the ocean, struggled to survive and got the family started. The second generation, the children of the immigrants, learned the American ways and helped the family move up in the world.

The third generation became completely American. They seldom used the old language, if they even knew it at all. These grandchildren of immigrants were the ones who finally saw the immigrants' dream come true.

The immigrants came to America and made it what it is. They remembered the old country but reached out to build a new life in a new land. For all the hardships and disappointment, the immigrants found what they came for in America.

In New York Harbor, near Ellis Island, is the Statue of Liberty. Many immigrants saw the statue as they came to America and knew that they could start a new life here.

The Statue of Liberty was a sign of welcome and a promise of opportunity. The poem on the statue reads

Give me your tired, your poor,
Your huddled masses yearning to breathe free. . . .
Send these, the homeless, . . . to me,
I lift my lamp beside the golden door!

FOR FURTHER READING

Day, Carl Olsen and Edmund Day. *The New Immigrants.* New York: Franklin Watts, 1985

Fisher, Leonard Everett. *Ellis Island: Gateway to the New World.* New York: Dutton, 1980

Fleming, Thomas J. *The Golden Door: the Story of American Immigration.* New York: Grosset and Dunlap, 1988

Freedman, Russell. *Immigrant Kids.* New York: Dutton, 1980

Hargrove, Jim. *Gateway to Freedom.* Chicago: Children's Press, 1986

INDEX

ABOUT THE AUTHOR

William J. Evitts was born in Chicago, Illinois, raised in Arlington, Virginia, and educated in the public schools there.

A 1964 graduate of Johns Hopkins University, Evitts went on to an M.A. at the University of Virginia and a doctorate in history at Hopkins. He was chairman of the History department at Hollins College (Virginia) for fifteen years before assuming his present post as the Director of Alumni Relations at Hopkins.

He is married and has two children. This is Evitts's third book, his second for young people.

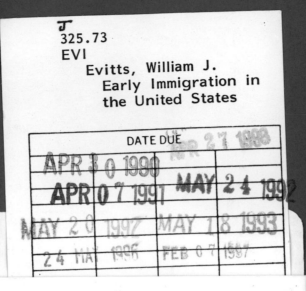